Find It in Nature!

# Flowers

by Jenna Lee Gleisner

Bullfrog Books

## Ideas for Parents and Teachers

Bullfrog Books let children practice reading informational text at the earliest reading levels. Repetition, familiar words, and photo labels support early readers.

### Before Reading

- Discuss the cover photo. What does it tell them?
- Look at the picture glossary together. Read and discuss the words.

### Read the Book

- "Walk" through the book and look at the photos. Let the child ask questions. Point out the photo labels.
- Read the book to the child, or have him or her read independently.

### After Reading

- Prompt the child to think more. Ask: Flower petals can be many different colors. What kinds of flowers have you seen? What color were their petals?

Bullfrog Books are published by Jump!
5357 Penn Avenue South
Minneapolis, MN 55419
www.jumplibrary.com



Library of Congress Cataloging-in-Publication Data

Names: Gleisner, Jenna Lee, author.
Title: Flowers / by Jenna Lee Gleisner.
Description: Minneapolis, MN: Jump!, Inc., [2024]
Series: Find it in nature! | Includes index.
Audience: Ages 5–8
Identifiers: LCCN 2023024613 (print)
LCCN 2023024614 (ebook)
ISBN 9798889966777 (hardcover)
ISBN 9798889966784 (paperback)
ISBN 9798889966791 (ebook)
Subjects: LCSH: Flowers—Juvenile literature.
Botany—Juvenile literature.
Classification: LCC QK49 .G5624 2024 (print)
LCC QK49 (ebook)
DDC 581—dc23/eng/20230525
LC record available at https://lccn.loc.gov/2023024613
LC ebook record available at https://lccn.loc.gov/2023024614

Editor: Katie Chanez
Designer: Molly Ballanger

Photo Credits: Vilor/Shutterstock, cover; Africa Studio/Shutterstock, 1; Scisetti Alfio/Shutterstock, 3; Elizabeth C Waters/Shutterstock, 4; Nathanael Siders/Shutterstock, 5, 23tm; Christopher O'Donnell/Shutterstock, 6–7, 23tr; Kristine Rad/Shutterstock, 7; Alesikka/Shutterstock, 8, 22tr, 23bm; pressdigital/iStock, 8–9; Cherishhh/Shutterstock, 10; joloei/Shutterstock, 11, 23br; Ancha Chiangmai/Shutterstock, 12–13; Kokhanchikov/Shutterstock, 14; Ethan Daniels/Shutterstock, 15, 23bl; Zheltyshev/Shutterstock, 16–17; Kisialiou Yury/Shutterstock, 17, 22bl, 23tl; Bakhtiyor Mardonov/Shutterstock, 18–19; Cavan Images/Getty, 20–21; Ian 2010/Shutterstock, 22tl; Sarycheva Olesia/Shutterstock, 22tml; New Africa/Shutterstock, 22tmr; Quang Ho/Shutterstock, 22bml, 22br; Nattika/Shutterstock, 22bmr; Marek Mierzejewski/Shutterstock, 24.

Printed in the United States of America at Corporate Graphics in North Mankato, Minnesota.

# Table of Contents

# Many Colors

A bee is on a flower.
The flower is purple.

It has a dome.
It is a coneflower.
Let's find more!

petal

Sunflowers are tall.
They have yellow petals.
They grow seeds.

Roses grow on bushes.
Watch out!
They have thorns.

Morning glories grow on vines.

They close at night.

They open in the morning!

Tiger lilies are orange.

They have brown.

Like a tiger!

Water lilies grow in water.

They have long stems.
They reach the bottom.

Look!

Tulips grow in snow!

They bloom in spring.

Daffodils do, too.
They have trumpets.
Bees stop by.

trumpet

Flowers are pretty.

They smell nice.

*Mmm!*

What kinds grow
near you?

# Match the Flower

**Match each flower with its name. Look back at the book if you need help!**

coneflower

rose

morning glory

tiger lily

water lily

tulip

daffodil

sunflower

# Picture Glossary

**bloom**
To produce flowers.

**dome**
A top shaped like half of a sphere.

**petals**
The colored outer parts of a flower.

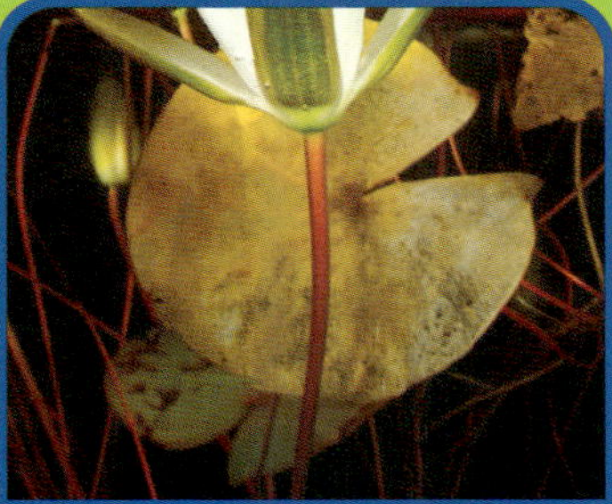

**stems**
The main parts of plants from which leaves and flowers grow.

**thorns**
Sharp points that stick out from a plant's stem.

**vines**
Plants with long stems that grow along the ground or climb.

# Index

# To Learn More

**Finding more information is as easy as 1, 2, 3.**

1. Go to www.factsurfer.com
2. Enter "flowers" into the search box.
3. Choose your book to see a list of websites.